INFOGRAPHIC
TOP
10

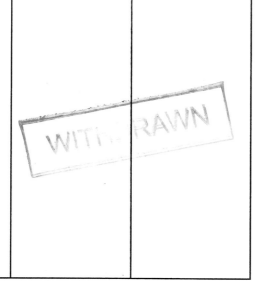

WAYLAND

CONTENTS

pages 8–9
See which birds have the largest wings and how they use them.

pages 18–19
Discover which animals make the loudest sounds and why.

WELCOME!

From the deadliest to the loudest and from the largest to the fastest, this book looks at the amazing record-breakers of the animal kingdom. It uses stunning icons, graphics and visualisations to show you how these amazing creatures raise the bar in the natural world.

pages 12–13
See how big bugs can grow.

Life size!

pages 4–5
Read about which animals would win in a sprint race.

SPEED ACROSS THE GROUND

<‹ ·· ›>

Some animals have evolved the amazing ability to run at breath-taking speed. Many of them can sprint short distances to chase down prey, while others can run fast to outpace and dodge any chasing predators.

PREDATOR VS PREY

Animals move quickly for two reasons – either to kill or to avoid being killed. However, not every animal can run for long distances. Cheetahs may be able to run very quickly, but they can sprint for only about 550 metres. At this point, they become too hot and too tired, and need to rest.

10 **8** **8** **6** **7** **5** **4**

Galloping horses

Fast-running, four-legged animals use their legs in sequence to push themselves as fast as possible. A horse's gallop begins with the two back feet pushing off the ground, one after the other. For a short period, the horse is off the ground, before the front two legs touch down.

FASTEST LAND ANIMALS

1. **Cheetah 120 km/h**
2. **Pronghorn 88.5 km/h**
3. **Springbok 88 km/h**
4. **Wildebeest 80.5 km/h**
5. **Lion 80 km/h**
6. **Greyhound 74 km/h**
7. **Jackrabbit 72 km/h**
=8. **African wild dog 71 km/h**
=8. **Kangaroo 71 km/h**
10. **Horse 70 km/h**

Fastest human: 44.7 km/h recorded during a 100-m-sprint (average speed between 60–80 m) by Usain Bolt.

Extending strides

Cheetahs are the sprint kings of the animal world. They have lightweight, slim bodies, which are perfect for life in the fast lane. Another key feature is a very flexible spine. This allows the cheetah to take enormous strides, each up to 8 m long, making it incredibly fast.

Spine compressed

Spine extended

SPEED IN THE WATER

It is much harder to move quickly through water than air, because water is far more dense. To swim quickly, super-fast fish need to have sleek, streamlined bodies and amazingly strong muscles.

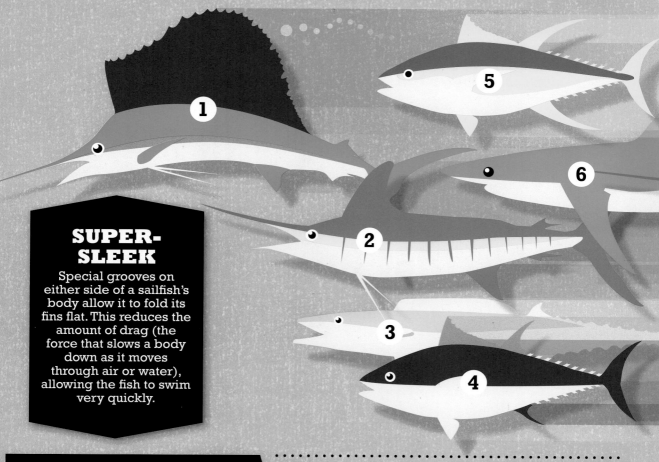

SUPER-SLEEK

Special grooves on either side of a sailfish's body allow it to fold its fins flat. This reduces the amount of drag (the force that slows a body down as it moves through air or water), allowing the fish to swim very quickly.

How far in 1 second?

This chart shows how far these different animals can swim in a single second compared to humans.

Fish – sailfish – 31 m
Mammal – common dolphin – 17 m
Reptile – green sea turtle – 15.6 m
Bird – gentoo penguin – 9.8 m
Amphibian – axolotl – 4.5 m
Human – 2.34 m
Invertebrate – whirligig beetle – 1.44 m

FASTEST SWIMMING ANIMALS

1. **Sailfish 112 km/h**
2. Striped marlin 80 km/h
3. **Wahoo 77 km/h**
4. Southern blue fin tuna 76 km/h
5. **Yellow fin tuna 74 km/h**
6. Blue shark 69 km/h
=7. **Bonefish 64 km/h**
=7. Swordfish 64 km/h
9. **Tarpon 56 km/h**
10. Tiger shark 53 km/h

Humans can swim at 8.45 km/h. This is the average speed of an Olympic 50-m freestyle swimmer.

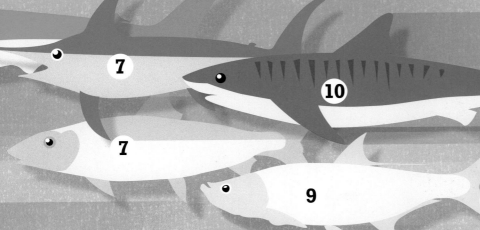

Convergent evolution

Fish have fins to push and steer them through the water. Other animals have body parts that look and work like fins – swimming birds have fin-shaped wings, while swimming mammals have flippers. The development of similar body parts by different animals is called convergent evolution.

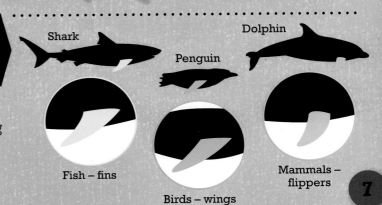

Shark

Dolphin

Penguin

Fish – fins

Birds – wings

Mammals – flippers

BIGGEST WINGSPAN

How birds soar

Bearded vulture

Bearded vultures are found throughout mountainous regions of Europe, Africa and Asia.

=5

3 metres

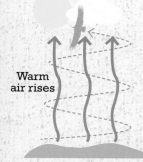

Warm air rises

Cool air descends

Many birds use their elongated wings to catch rising currents of warm air, called thermals, to push them high into the air. From here, the birds look out for signs of another thermal, before gliding over to it so they can be pushed up again.

Griffon vulture

These birds live in colonies high up on cliffs. From here, they can fly out and search for dead animals to feed on.

=7

2.8 metres

California condor

The California condor uses rising air currents to soar up to altitudes of 4,500 m or more.

=7

2.8 metres

Golden eagle

These birds build huge nests, which are known as eyries.

=9

2.5 metres

Grey crowned crane

These birds use large inflatable sacs beneath their chins to produce loud, booming calls.

=9

2.5 metres

=3 Marabou stork

Marabou storks feed mainly on dead animals, but they will catch live prey during the breeding season.

3.4 metres

=1 Wandering albatross

These giant birds use their enormous wings to glide over the ocean for hours without having to flap them.

3.6 metres

=5 Whooper swan

These birds migrate for hundreds of kilometres in large 'V' formations.

3 metres

=3 Andean condor

These heavy birds can weigh up to 15 kg and need thermals or winds to help them into the air.

3.4 metres

=1 Great white pelican

A great white pelican will eat up to 1.5 kg of fish every single day.

3.6 metres

WORLD OF GIANTS

Giant creatures have many advantages over small ones. Being big and strong makes it easier to defeat other animals, while being tall makes it easier to reach out-of-the-way food. Large animals are also better insulated against extreme heat and cold.

The figure by each human silhouette represents the number of adult humans each animal weighs.

BLUE WHALE

All 10 of these animals together are less than half the weight of the biggest animal to have ever lived – the blue whale. This giant can weigh around 200 tonnes.

• Its heart weighs about 700 kg – as much as 10 people.
• Its lung capacity is 5,000 litres – enough to fill 62.5 baths
• It blows air and mucus out of its blow hole to a height of 12 metres – about twice the height of a giraffe.

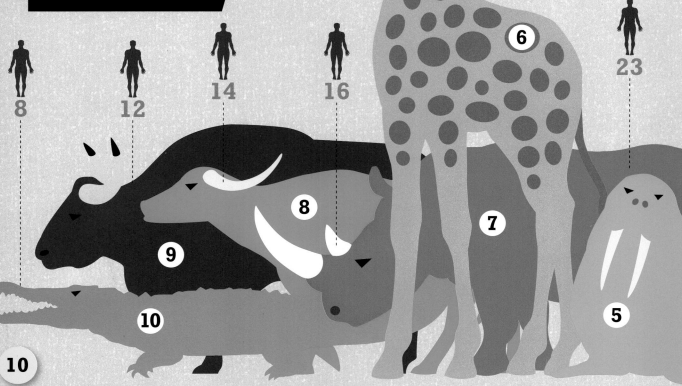

18

8

12

14

16

6

23

9

8

7

10

5

HEAVIEST LAND ANIMALS

1. **African elephant – 5.25 tonnes**
2. **Asian elephant – 3.5 tonnes**
3. **White rhinoceros – 2.5 tonnes**
4. **Hippopotamus – 2.3 tonnes**
5. **Walrus – 1.6 tonnes**
6. **Giraffe – 1.25 tonnes**
7. **Black rhinoceros – 1.15 tonnes**
8. **Wild Asian water buffalo – 0.98 tonnes**
9. **Gaur – 0.85 tonnes**
10. **Saltwater crocodile – 0.6 tonnes**

Humans weigh 70 kg (0.07 tonnes) on average, but the heaviest person was Joe Brower Minnoch who weighed more than 635 kg (0.635 tonnes).

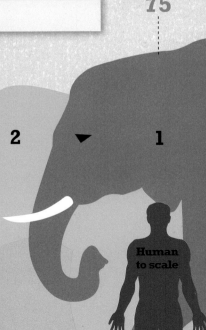

75

50

33

35

2

1

3

4

Human to scale

BIG BUGS

<-->

Insects are some of the most successful forms of life on Earth and make up about half of all species on the planet. They all have a tough outer skeleton and six jointed legs.

Life size!

④

②

⑩

⑤

WORLD'S SMALLEST INSECT

The world's smallest insect is the fairyfly. Males of a species from Costa Rica measure just 0.139 mm long, which is less than half the width of the full stop at the end of this sentence.

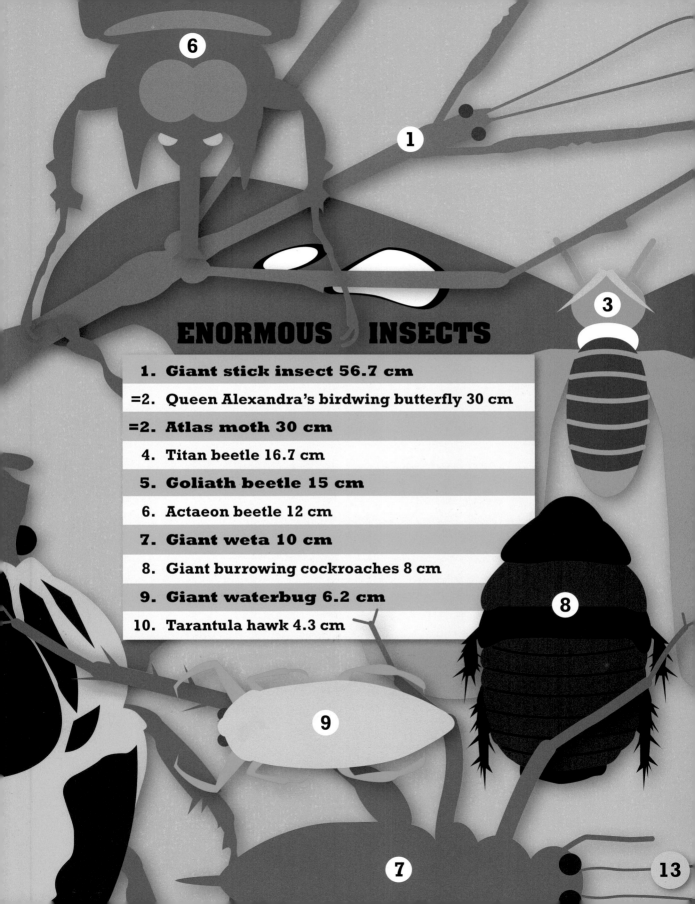

ENORMOUS INSECTS

1. **Giant stick insect 56.7 cm**
=2. **Queen Alexandra's birdwing butterfly 30 cm**
=2. **Atlas moth 30 cm**
4. **Titan beetle 16.7 cm**
5. **Goliath beetle 15 cm**
6. **Actaeon beetle 12 cm**
7. **Giant weta 10 cm**
8. **Giant burrowing cockroaches 8 cm**
9. **Giant waterbug 6.2 cm**
10. **Tarantula hawk 4.3 cm**

NASTY GNASHERS!

The hardest parts of your body are your teeth. These tough mouth parts are designed to tear off food and crush it up so that our bodies can absorb nutrients. Other teeth are used for fighting and to kill any prey.

Teeth types

Animal teeth can be long and pointed for fighting and grasping, sharp like scissors for slicing through meat, or flat and tough to grind up plant food.

Molars
These are used for grinding food.

Tusks
Tusks are teeth that are so long, they stick out of the mouth. They are used for fighting and rummaging for food.

Carnassials
Carnivores have these scissor-like teeth for slicing through meat and bone.

Canines
Located at the front of the mouth, these long, sharp teeth are used to grasp prey.

Snake fangs

Some snakes kill their prey by injecting them with a deadly venom, delivered through needle-sharp fangs. The long fangs have a canal running through them. As the snake bites into its prey, venom is pushed through these canals and into the victim's body.

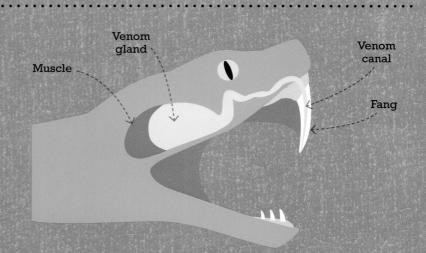

Venom gland

Venom canal

Muscle

Fang

LONGEST ANIMAL TEETH

1. **African elephant tusks – 3 m**
2. Narwhal tusk – 2.7 m
3. **Asian elephant tusks – 2.4 m**
4. Walrus tusks – 90 cm
5. **Hippopotamus teeth – 40 cm**
6. Babirusa tusks – 30 cm
7. **Warthog tusks – 25.5 cm**
8. Sperm whale teeth – 18 cm
9. **Payara fangs – 15 cm**
10. Lion canines – 9 cm

The longest human tooth measured 3.2 cm. It was extracted from the mouth of Loo Hui Jing of Singapore in 2009.

Animals with the most teeth

A human child usually has 24 teeth, and an adult will replace these with 32 teeth.

The record for the human with the most teeth was a boy in India who had 232 extracted in 2014.

But even this is nothing compared to the record-breakers of the animal kingdom.

Sharks can have 20,000 teeth throughout their life – they are replaced regularly.

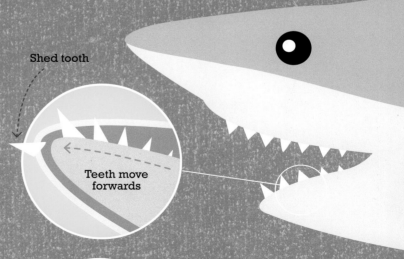

Shed tooth

Teeth move forwards

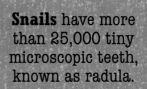

Snails have more than 25,000 tiny microscopic teeth, known as radula.

MANY HAPPY RETURNS

50 years

quahog dies 2006

2000

1945 – World War II ends

1900

1876 – Alexander Graham Bell invents the telephone

1800

1776 – Declaration of Independence creates the USA

1700

1616 – William Shakespeare dies

1600

1506 – Leonardo da Vinci paints the Mona Lisa

1500

quahog born 1499

Record breaker

The longest-living creature was an ocean quahog (a type of mussel) that was 507 years old when it was killed accidentally by scientists in 2006. It was born in 1499.

Growth ring

Scientists can tell the age of a quahog by counting the growth rings in the creature's shell – just like the growth rings in a tree trunk.

0 years

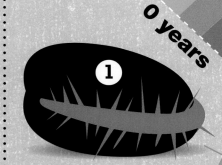

400 years

350 years

LONGEST LIVING ANIMALS

1. **Ocean quahog – 500 years**
2. Bowhead whale – 211 years
3. **Rougheye rockfish – 205 years**
4. Red sea urchin – 200 years
5. **Galapagos tortoise – 177 years**
6. Shortraker rockfish – 157 years
=7. **Lake sturgeon – 152 years**
=7. Aldabara giant tortoise – 152 years
9. **Orange roughy – 149 years**
10. Warty oreo – 140 years

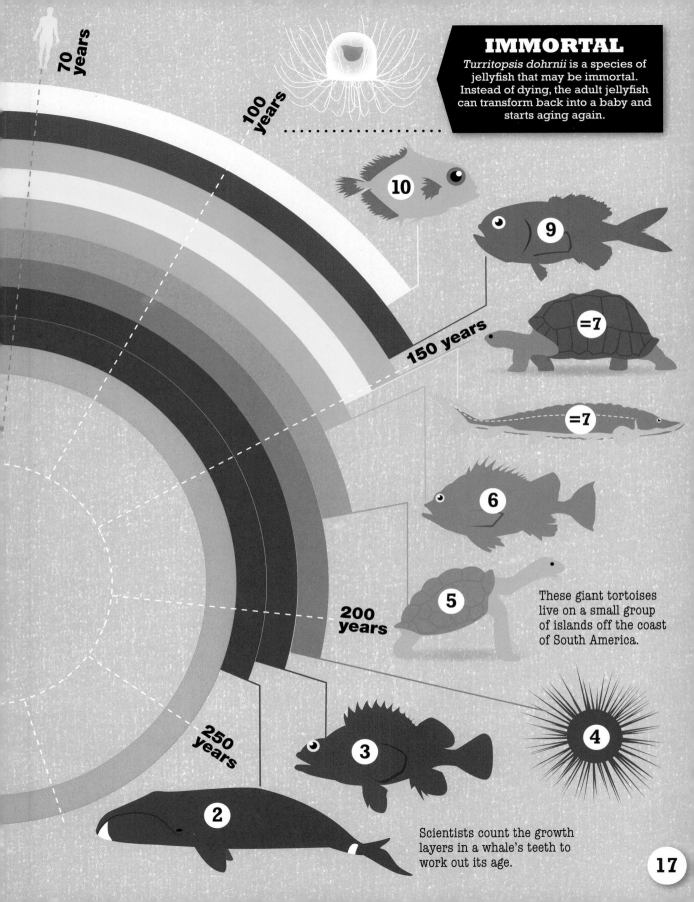

70 years

100 years

IMMORTAL

Turritopsis dohrnii is a species of jellyfish that may be immortal. Instead of dying, the adult jellyfish can transform back into a baby and starts aging again.

10

9

150 years

=7

=7

6

5

200 years

These giant tortoises live on a small group of islands off the coast of South America.

4

250 years

3

2

Scientists count the growth layers in a whale's teeth to work out its age.

17

LOUDEST ANIMALS

Some whales can produce sounds that could travel more than 2,600 km in ideal conditions. That's almost the distance from Chicago to Los Angeles. However, modern noise pollution limits this distance.

LOUD BANG

By clicking one of its claws, a tiger pistol shrimp creates a 'bubble bullet' that bursts and stuns prey. The extreme pressure caused by the bubble also creates a flash of light indicating very high temperatures. Scientists believe the temperature inside the bubble can reach nearly 5,500°C – that's as hot as the surface of the Sun!

1

Tiger pistol shrimp

This tiny crustacean makes the loudest noise in the animal world as it clicks its claws.

200dB

dB

0

20 40 60

80

SILENCE

A WHISPER

NORMAL CONVERSATION

200

2

Blue whale

The largest animal on the planet makes low frequency sounds which scientists believe are used to attract mates.

188 dB

190

VOLCANO ERUPTION

180

ROCKET LAUNCH

170

160

Echolocation

Echoes bounce back

Some animals, such as dolphins and bats, use sounds to detect prey. They send out high-pitched sounds, called ultrasound, which bounce back off any prey, telling the predator where its prey is.

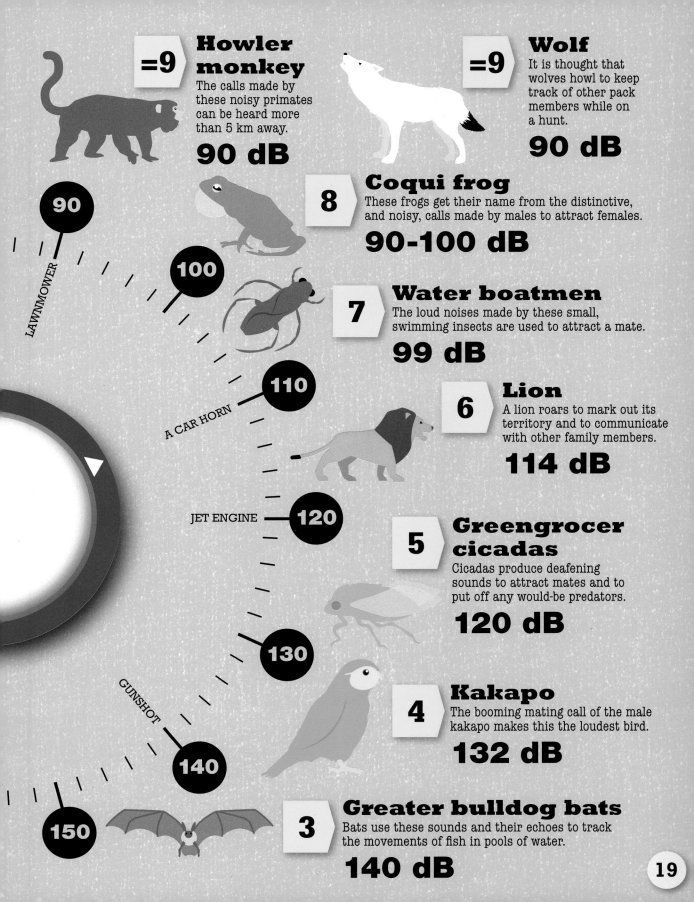

Howler monkey

=9

The calls made by these noisy primates can be heard more than 5 km away.

90 dB

Wolf

=9

It is thought that wolves howl to keep track of other pack members while on a hunt.

90 dB

Coqui frog

8

These frogs get their name from the distinctive, and noisy, calls made by males to attract females.

90-100 dB

Water boatmen

7

The loud noises made by these small, swimming insects are used to attract a mate.

99 dB

Lion

6

A lion roars to mark out its territory and to communicate with other family members.

114 dB

Greengrocer cicadas

5

Cicadas produce deafening sounds to attract mates and to put off any would-be predators.

120 dB

Kakapo

4

The booming mating call of the male kakapo makes this the loudest bird.

132 dB

Greater bulldog bats

3

Bats use these sounds and their echoes to track the movements of fish in pools of water.

140 dB

LAWNMOWER

A CAR HORN

JET ENGINE

GUNSHOT

90 · 100 · 110 · 120 · 130 · 140 · 150

MOVING ANIMALS

Many animals travel thousands of kilometres every year looking for places to eat, to mate and to give birth and raise young. This movement is called migration.

384,400 km

Grey whale

5

1

Arctic tern

4

7

Globe skimmer dragonfly

Northern elephant seal

Common tern

3

LAND MIGRATION

The largest land migration is made by blue wildebeest. More than 1.3 million of these animals take part in this annual migration – that's the same as the population of San Diego, California.

Humpback whale

9

LONGEST ANNUAL MIGRATIONS

1. **Arctic tern – 70,000 km**
2. Sooty shearwater – 64,000 km
3. **Common tern – 26,000 km**
4. Northern elephant seal – 21,000 km
5. **Grey whale – 20,000 km**
6. Leatherback turtle – 19,300 km
7. **Globe skimmer dragonflies – 15,000 km**
8. Bar-tailed godwit – 11,000 km
9. **Humpback whale – 8,300 km**
10. Tuna – 7,700 km

The Arctic tern follows a long figure-of-eight shape between the Arctic and Antarctic. This makes the journey more than four times the distance a direct route would be.

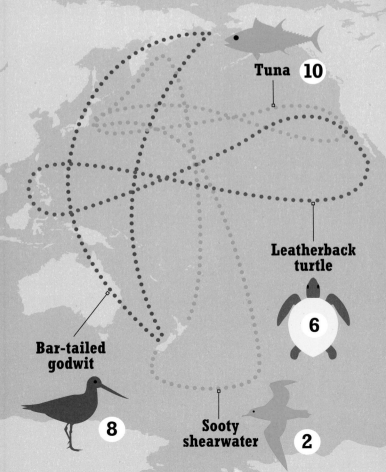

Tuna **10**

Leatherback turtle **6**

Bar-tailed godwit **8**

Sooty shearwater **2**

Caribou

One of the longest migrations on land is made by caribou. They travel about 5,000 km every year – that's the same as the distance from Paris to Beijing.

x44

To prepare for its migration, a caribou will eat about 5 kg of food every day during the summer, which is the same weight as 44 burgers!

Every day, billions of tiny creatures called zooplankton migrate up towards the ocean surface and down again in a movement called vertical migration.

Up and down

THE BIG SLEEP

Some animals spend part of the year in a long sleep-like period called hibernation, when food and water are in short supply and the conditions are harsh. These pages list some of the longest hibernators.

3

J F M A
✗ ✗ ✗ ✗
✗ ✗ ✗ D

Fat-tailed dwarf lemur
During hibernation, these lemurs lose 50 per cent of their weight.
7 months

1

✗ ✗ ✗ ✗
✗ J J A
S ✗ ✗ ✗

Alpine marmot
During hibernation, this mammal's heart rate slows from 120 beats per minute (bpm) to just 4 bpm.
8 months

2

✗ ✗ ✗ ✗
M J J A
✗ ✗ ✗ ✗

Bumblebee (queen)
The queen bee is the only one that sleeps through the winter – all the other bees die. After the winter, the queen wakes up and starts to lay eggs to re-form the hive.
6–8 months

4

✗ ✗ ✗ A
M J J A
✗ ✗ ✗ ✗

Wood frog
These amphibians produce a natural 'anti-freeze' to protect themselves through the cold winter months.
7 months

Summer sleep
While some animals hibernate during cold, winter months, other creatures enter a similar state when conditions are very warm and dry. This condition is called aestivation and it stops animals

5

Arctic ground squirrel

These mammals shelter in small burrows dug into the tundra.

6 months

6

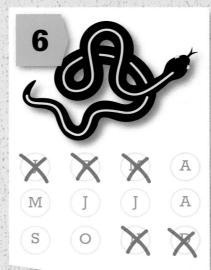

Garter snake

These snakes hibernate in huge groups to keep each other warm.

5 months

7

Hedgehog

If the weather gets too cold during hibernation, a hedgehog wakes up and moves to a warmer place.

4–5 months

=8

Common poorwill

This is the only known bird species to hibernate through the winter.

3–4 months

=8

Black bear

For more than 100 days during hibernation, bears will not eat, drink, urinate or defecate.

3–4 months

10

Big brown bat

During hibernation, this bat's heart rate will drop from 1,000 bpm to just 25 bpm.

2 months

from drying out. Creatures that do this include snails, beetles, tortoises and frogs.

PET PLANET

People have lived with animals for thousands of years – either for food and clothing, for working, to hunt, or just for good company. Over the years, we have created different breeds to produce animals with varying characteristics.

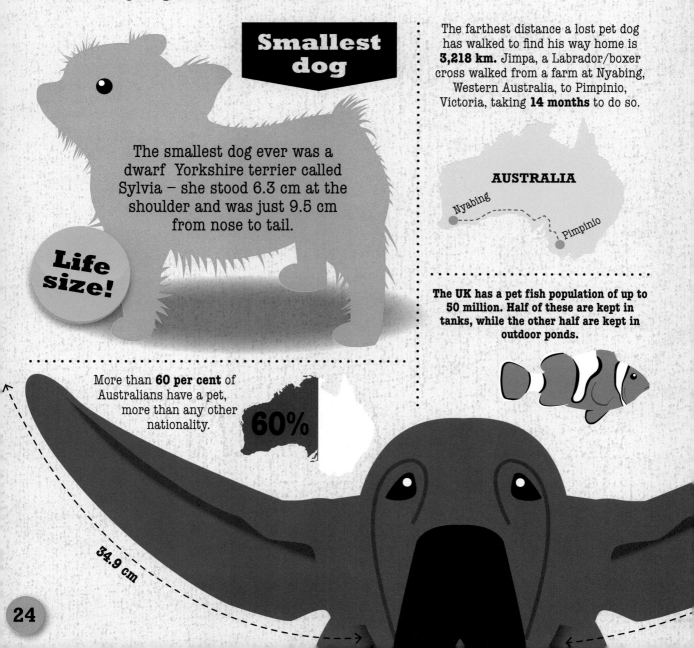

Smallest dog

The smallest dog ever was a dwarf Yorkshire terrier called Sylvia – she stood 6.3 cm at the shoulder and was just 9.5 cm from nose to tail.

Life size!

The farthest distance a lost pet dog has walked to find his way home is **3,218 km.** Jimpa, a Labrador/boxer cross walked from a farm at Nyabing, Western Australia, to Pimpinio, Victoria, taking **14 months** to do so.

AUSTRALIA

Nyabing

Pimpinio

The UK has a pet fish population of up to 50 million. Half of these are kept in tanks, while the other half are kept in outdoor ponds.

More than **60 per cent** of Australians have a pet, more than any other nationality.

60%

34.9 cm

COUNTRIES WITH THE MOST PET CATS

1. USA – 76,430,000
2. China – 53,100,000
3. Russia – 12,700,000
4. Brazil – 12,466,000
5. France – 9,600,000
6. Italy – 9,400,000
=7. UK – 7,700,000
=7. Germany – 7,700,000
9. Ukraine – 7,350,000
10. Japan – 7,300,000

With more than 76 million cats, the USA has one cat for every four people

Largest litter

19

The largest litter by a domestic cat is **19**. In comparison, the average litter size is just **4–6**.

Longest ears

Tigger the bloodhound holds the record for the longest dog ears ever. His right ear measured **34.9 cm** from head to tip and his left ear measured **34.2 cm**.

34.2 cm

10 9 =7 =7 6 5 4 3

1
2

KILLER CREATURES

The animals shown here are some of the deadliest on the planet and kill the most people every year. Some are ferocious predators, while others carry killer diseases.

In North America, more people are killed by deer (130 per year) than by grizzly bears (about 2.5 fatal attacks per year on average). Deer are involved in more than 1.5 million car crashes each year.

130 **v** 2.5

Surprisingly deadly

= 5,000 deaths per year

Dog (rabies)

The greatest risk from dogs is an infected bite. Rabies has a survival rate of less than 10 per cent.

3

25,000

Asian cobra

The powerful venom delivered in this snake's bite can cause heart failure and suffocation.

2

50,000

Tsetse fly (sleeping sickness)

This blood-sucking fly carries a parasite which causes the deadly sleeping sickness.

=4

10,000

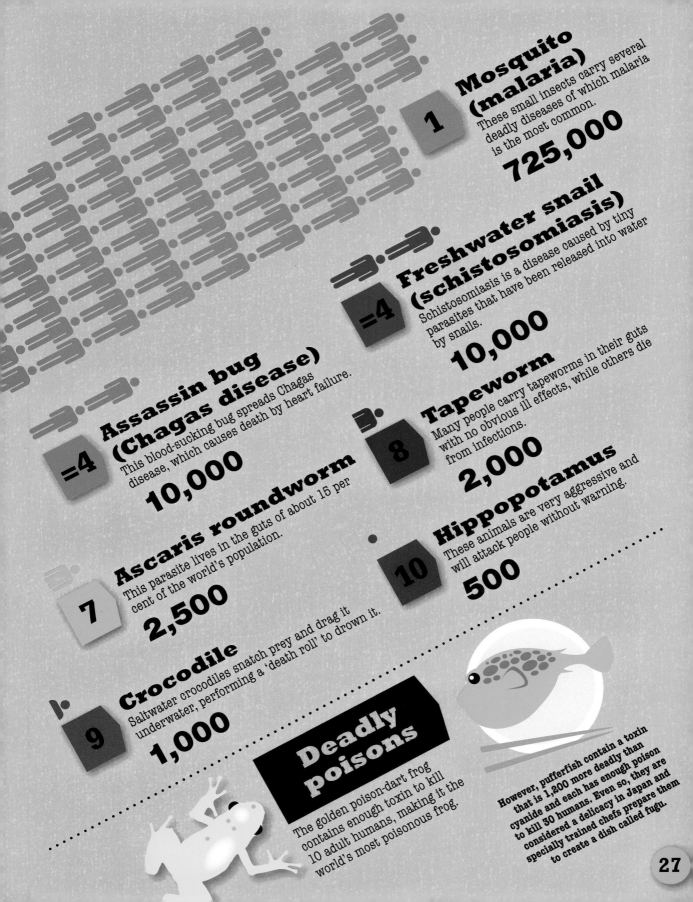

Mosquito (malaria)

1

These small insects carry several deadly diseases of which malaria is the most common.

725,000

Freshwater snail (schistosomiasis)

=4

Schistosomiasis is a disease caused by tiny parasites that have been released into water by snails.

10,000

Assassin bug (Chagas disease)

=4

This blood-sucking bug spreads Chagas disease, which causes death by heart failure.

10,000

Tapeworm

8

Many people carry tapeworms in their guts with no obvious ill effects, while others die from infections.

2,000

Ascaris roundworm

7

This parasite lives in the guts of about 15 per cent of the world's population.

2,500

Hippopotamus

10

These animals are very aggressive and will attack people without warning.

500

Crocodile

9

Saltwater crocodiles snatch prey and drag it underwater, performing a 'death roll' to drown it.

1,000

Deadly poisons

The golden poison-dart frog contains enough toxin to kill 10 adult humans, making it the world's most poisonous frog.

However, pufferfish contain a toxin that is 1,200 more deadly than cyanide and each has enough poison to kill 30 humans. Even so, they are considered a delicacy in Japan and specially trained chefs prepare them to create a dish called fugu.

ANIMALS UNDER THREAT

Changes in the environment, such as global warming and habitat loss, can threaten an animal's existence. If that change is great enough, it can push whole species to the brink of extinction.

Habitat loss

By 2100, it is predicted that annual sea ice will have declined by 10–50 per cent and summer sea ice will have decreased by 50–100 per cent. This will affect the habitat of polar bears and reduce their numbers by 30 per cent.

Current population 25,000

Projected population 17,500

2100

2014

50%

In the last 100 years, about half of all coral reefs...

70%

... and nearly one-third of mangrove forests have been lost.

MOST ENDANGERED ANIMALS (NUMBER LEFT)

=1. **Ivory-billed woodpecker – may be extinct**

=1. **Saola – may be extinct**

3. **Northern sportive lemur – 18**

4. **Amur leopard – 20**

5. **Javan rhinoceros – 40**

6. **North Pacific Right Whale – 50**

7. **White-headed langur – < 70**

8. **Vaquita – 100–300**

9. **Cross river gorilla – 200–300**

10. **Sumatran tiger – 441–679**

Some scientists believe that animal species are becoming extinct faster than new species are being discovered.

Climate change

The UN Climate Panel states that an increase in the average global temperature of just 1°C will lead to an increasing risk of extinction for 30 per cent of species on Earth.

13°C (average temperature)

1°C increase

30 per cent

3 species per hour

According to the UN Convention on Biological Diversity, three species are becoming extinct each hour. This extinction rate is the fastest in Earth's history.

Ticking clock

GLOSSARY

aestivation
A sleep-like state that some creatures enter into during very warm and dry periods. It stops the animals drying out.

breeding season
A period during the year when animals look and compete for mates and to have young.

carnassials
Type of teeth that are sharp and come together in a slicing action, like scissors, to cut up flesh and bones.

canines
Long, pointed teeth that are found at the front of the mouths of carnivores (meat-eaters) and omnivores (animals that eat plants and meat). They are used to hold food.

cartilage
A flexible tissue that supports some body parts, such as the human nose and ear, or, in some cases, is used to support the entire body, such as sharks and other cartilaginous fish.

convergent evolution
When different types of animal or plant develop features or behaviour that fulfil the same role. It can be seen in the shape and function of fins in fish, wings in swimming birds and flippers in aquatic mammals, all of which have the same shape and help the animals to swim.

decibel
The unit used to measure the intensity or volume (loudness) of sound.

drag
The force that slows down objects as they move through air or water.

echolocation
The use of sound to detect objects. Whales and bats send out sounds and listen for the echoes that bounce off objects, including prey.

extinction
When a type of living thing dies out completely and is no longer present.

galloping
A fast style of movement made by four-legged animals, such as a horse.

hibernation
A sleep-like state that some animals enter into during winter months, when food and water are in short supply. The rate at which the body operates slows down, saving energy.

insulated
When something is protected from changes in temperature,whether it is extreme heat or extreme cold.

migrate
To move from one place to another. Animals migrate to avoid harsh conditions, to search for food and water, or to go somewhere suitable to raise young.

molars
Large flat teeth that are found near the backs of the mouths of animals, and are used to grind food up while chewing.

predator
An animal that hunts other animals to eat.

prey
An animal that is hunted by other animals for food.

radula
A tooth-like structure found in molluscs, such as snails, that is used for tearing and scraping food.

sprint
A fast style of running that can only be done for a short distance.

streamlined
When something has a shape that helps it to move through air or water as easily as possible.

thermal
A rising current of warm air.

tusks
Extra-long teeth that stick out from the mouth and are used in fighting or foraging for food.

ultrasound
Sounds that are so high-pitched that they cannot be heard by humans.

WEBSITES

MORE INFO:

http://nationalzoo.si.edu/Animals/AnimalRecords
Find out which animals hold which records in this section of the Smithsonian Institution's website.

http://www.guinnessworldrecords.com
The website for all things regarding record-breaking. It is packed with thousands of world records and facts.

http://www.bbc.co.uk/nature/collections/p00hldcc
Videos and facts from the BBC's Natural History unit.

MORE GRAPHICS:

www.visualinformation.info
A website that contains a whole host of infographic material on subjects as diverse as natural history, science, sport and computer games.

www.coolinfographics.com
A collection of infographics and data visualisations from other online resources, magazines and newspapers.

www.dailyinfographic.com
A comprehensive collection of infographics on an enormous range of topics that is updated every day!

INDEX

<·····························>

Acknowledgements

First published in 2016 by Wayland
Copyright © Wayland 2016
All rights reserved.

Wayland, an imprint of
Hachette Children's Group
Part of Hodder & Stoughton
Carmelite House
50 Victoria Embankment
London EC4Y 0DZ

MIX
Paper from
responsible sources
FSC® C104740

Series editor: Julia Adams

Produced by Tall Tree Ltd
Editor: Jon Richards
Designer: Ed Simkins

Dewey classification: 590-dc23
ISBN: 9780750297653
Library ebook ISBN: 9780750287548

Printed in China

An Hachette UK company

www.hachette.co.uk
www.hachettechildrens.co.uk

The website addresses (URLs)
included in this book were valid
at the time of going to press.
However, because of the nature
of the Internet, it is possible that
some addresses may have
changed, or sites may have
changed or closed down, since
publication. While the author
and Publisher regret any
inconvenience this may cause
the readers, no responsibility
for any such changes can be
accepted by either the author
or the Publisher.